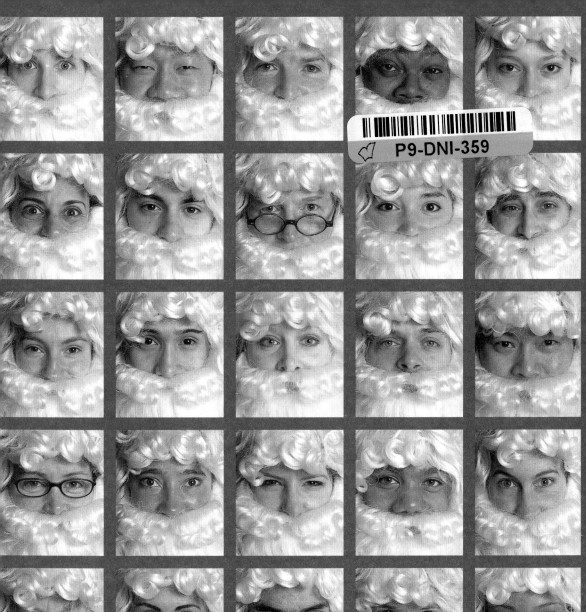
P9-DNI-359

HOW TO BE
SANTA CLAUS

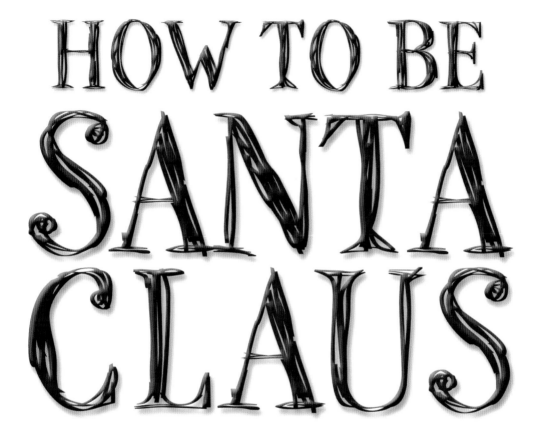

HOW TO BE SANTA CLAUS

nick kelsh

STEWART, TABORI & CHANG

NEW YORK

I'm not proud of this photograph, but it's where I will begin.

I have no choice—it's all I have. It's all you have.

I am missing some hair. I'm on my second marriage.
I have no upper-body strength and one day doctors will
replace my right knee. My son is well aware that his father
is less than perfect.

But last Christmas Eve I was Santa Claus—and it made
a difference.

Another you

You are Santa Claus when you decide to be the person you have always been.

You will eagerly look for ways to be thoughtful. You will be generous in ways you once thought impossible or even inappropriate.

After all, is there anything more irrational than delivering a gift to every child in the world in one December night? To say nothing of your mode of transportation.

Being Santa is being someone else. That someone else is you.

DON'T OVERCOOK GETTING A GOOD PHOTO OF YOUR SELF... COMMON MISTAKE.

DRAW ATTENTION TO THE EYES. THAT'S WHAT THIS IS ALL ABOUT.

YOU WILL LIKELY N[EED] AGE YOURSELF/VISU[AL] I USED HOUSE PAINT FOR EYEBROWS..... BIG REGRET. (I SUGGEST WATER-BASE[D]

AVOID ANY MATERIAL THAT FEELS OR LOOKS ARTIFICIAL. POP FOR THE GOOD HAT.

LOOK LIKE SANTA.... FEEL LIKE SANTA.

MY WIFE THIN[KS] CURLY LOC[KS] ONE IS A NICE I THINK IT'[S] LITTLE MUCH WHATEVE[R]

THINK OF YOUR FACE AS ONE BIG SMILE.

BLUE EYES DON'T HURT. IF YOU'VE GOT THEM, FLAUNT THEM! BUT COLOR MAKES NO DIFFERENCE. EYE CONTACT IS EVERYTHING.

ABSOLUTELY BE PERFECT WHITE.

CONSIDER TRIMMING YOUR BEARD TO MAKE YOUR MOUTH VISIBLE

A LITTLE LIPSTICK HERE... THE RED COLOR COMPLIMENTS THE HAT AND REINFORCES THE NORTH POLE THING.

I THINK THE STRING MAKES SOME KIND OF FASHION STATEMENT. I'M NOT SURE WHICH ONE BUT I THINK IT'S A NICE DETAIL. TAKE IT OR LEAVE IT.

...NICE BEARD IS [...] BEAR[D]

The face of Christmas future

Choose your role models carefully.

• Santa Claus does not sit on a throne on a float in a parade.

• Santa Claus is not the tired-looking man selling his image at the mall.

• Santa Claus is not a product of Madison Avenue.

• Santa Claus is a product of the heart.

And he has a good costume.

Straight to the heart

Santa Claus is well disguised. It is important that no one who meets Santa thinks he is someone else.

A good costume lets you park everything you've ever been at the door—you can be what you've always wanted to be.

But Santa's face can shine through only if you hide yours. Draw attention to his eyes. It is where children will enter.

Whisker shock

Becoming Santa is part imagination, part logistical hassle.

You will probably need to shop for a costume in a season known for shopping excess. You will spend money at a time when money is short.

A decent beard does not come cheap. You can cut corners everywhere else, but do not cut corners on Santa's face.

Becoming Santa can make a mess of your November. Being Santa can transform your December—if not your life.

Ground rules

Do these look like boots to you? They do not look like boots to me. More importantly, they do not look like boots to a child.

Santa Claus is a working man. He has a small herd of reindeer to care for. He has thousands of miles to travel. He has millions of children to make happy. He has a single night to accomplish his task.

Santa wears real boots.

The calorie conundrum

Santa Claus is fat. You would be too if you ate as many cookies as he does.

Santa's size is one of the reasons children love him. Do not disappoint them. If you are not naturally endowed, you may require a pillow or two.

Maintain the proper demeanor. Santa is well aware of how funny his big belly looks in a bright red suit. Santa does not take anyone, including himself, too seriously.

He loves the body that God gave him. If Santa worried about his weight, he would take up jogging. He prefers to travel by sleigh.

Creatures comfort

Spending time in a crowd of children is a situation many adults prefer to avoid. Fortunately, Santa Claus has a high tolerance for childish behavior.

But when Christmas is over, Santa eagerly anticipates the brunt of winter yet to come. It's when his reindeer will need him the most. He looks forward to spending frosty mornings with creatures that speak no human language. The man and the deer communicate with glances and smiles and nudges. Santa feeds their cold hungry bodies. The deer nurture Santa's spirit.

Santa loves animals almost as much as he loves children.

What if Santa's a woman?

She is a woman. She's a man, too.

Naughty or nice

Question: Was Santa Claus a good boy?

Hint: As a boy, he was almost always kind. He could be disruptive in class. Girls thought he was cute, even though he was not traditionally good looking. He was always attracted to the smart girls. He was easily distracted. He seemed incapable of guilt or regret. He liked sports well enough, but never excelled. It took him a while, but he learned to love to read. Once, when choosing sides for teams, he chose the slowest kid first instead of last. No one had ever done that before. He was really nice to his little brothers and sisters, although he did make them run errands for him when his parents weren't home. Right from the start, he liked to share. It took him a while to catch on to the importance of helping around the house, but as he grew older it became a habit for which his mother loved him. He was absolutely nutty for fireworks. Thanksgiving was—and is—his favorite holiday. He never lived up to what experts considered to be his potential. In short, he was always on the verge of having a little too much fun.

Answer: It depends on what your definition of good is.

Joy to the neighborhood

How did Santa Claus come to be?

Different cultures have different legends. Santa is charmed by them all.

This much we know for sure: There was a year (we don't know which one) when a man (we will never know his name) disguised himself in a red suit and beard.

Then he knocked on a neighbor's door, wanting nothing more than to have some fun and spread a little joy.

A beautiful thing

"Ho, ho, ho," is not a legitimate laugh. Any six-year-old can see through a bad ho, ho, ho.

Santa does not feel obligated to laugh—he laughs when he thinks something is funny. And when he thinks something is funny, he laughs till he's red in the face. Tears roll. He's left gasping for air.

It's a beautiful thing to watch.

Santa is not embarrassed to laugh at his own jokes. (This is common among people who love to laugh.)

Hey, Santa…

- Is that beard real?

  Yeah, real itchy.
- Why do you live at the North Pole?

  The South Pole struck me as a little bleak.
- How do you come down a chimney?

  Same way you go up except backwards.
- How much do you weigh?

  How much coal do you want in your stocking?
- What do you do the day after Christmas?

  I play with the naughty kids' toys.
- Would you like some milk and cookies?

  Does an elf wear felt?
- What do *you* want for Christmas?

  The simple joy of bringing happiness to children…and the Sleighmaster 5000 XE, silver blue.
- How can you be at every house in the world in one night?

  Who wants ice cream?
- Why didn't you bring me what I wanted last year?

  Last year you asked one too many questions. Anything else?

Defy the critics

People will scoff at you. It will bother you less
if you know why.

They are scared.

Dressing in a red suit and espousing a radical
philosophy—unlimited giving—is simply going to strike
some people as dangerous.

And, let's face it, you *are* peculiar. You will claim to have
entered the building though a chimney. You will tell
young children that you converse with flying deer.

So laugh at yourself. See the humor in your foolishness
—and the wisdom in it. This is not about you. It's about
sharing with others.

What's really humorous is that they are Santa Claus, too.
They just don't know it.

Out of the blue

For children, a surprise appearance by Santa Claus is unforgettable. For adults, it can be the highlight of a stressful, complicated season.

When you are Santa, consider appearing in places you will never, ever be expected. It could be a house across the street or a hospital across the continent.

Santa never calls ahead. Surprise gives strength to a magical being. Pretend you dropped from the clouds.

Return the kiss

When you become Santa Claus, expect to be kissed by a woman you have long considered kissable but have never considered kissing.

Do the right thing. Make her proud. Return the kiss.

Under any other circumstances this would be awkward. If she has children they will likely be watching. If she has a husband he could well be your close friend.

Return the kiss.

Watching the woman they love kiss a man they love will bring them great joy.

Getting what you want
is not really what you want

Not even Santa Claus can make people happy by giving them everything on their list—believe me, he's tried. The happiness proves fleeting—for both the giver and the receiver.

Santa's philosophy is simple: Thoughtfulness is the gift and the most thoughtful gifts are unexpected.

A thoughtful gift says, "I know you."

Santa gives at least one thoughtful gift per chimney.

The lesson of Henry

There were many people in the room who did not receive
a gift from Santa Claus when Henry received his guitar.
They didn't care. They knew how much Henry loves music.

Watching someone you love receive a thoughtful gift can
be better than receiving one yourself.

When you are Santa Claus, you don't need gifts for
everyone in the room—except for the children, of course.
Their sense of fairness is perfect and should not
be violated.

Grown-ups in toyland

Santa Claus understands the importance of taking life seriously. We should brush after every meal. We should buy low and sell high. We should check our oil regularly.

But there was a time in your life when you cared more about magic than logic. You cared about toys.

And then, as you developed an interest in the opposite sex, you coincidentally stopped receiving toys for Christmas. Clothes were the substitute.

Santa has no problem with the opposite sex, but he does have a problem with growing too old for toys. And he does not consider computer gadgets and food processors toys.

Balsa-wood airplanes and paper dolls are toys.

Toys can reconnect a grumpy grown-up with a playful spirit. As Santa, you will never have a better opportunity to soften a hard heart.

The value of small

Santa Claus is a large man who appreciates small things.

He loves stocking stuffers. The possibilities for expressing love with small, inexpensive gifts are endless.

Santa also loves tradition. Everyone gets an orange and a brand-new dime. The orange will go uneaten and the dime will disappear, but they will never be forgotten.

Humbug is humbug

There are intellectuals who could convincingly build the case that Santa Claus is silly and therefore, logically, anyone who wants to be Santa is a fool. They could argue the very concept of Santa Claus himself is not just benignly childish, but psychologically damaging and perhaps even abusive to our children. Their evidence is powerful and intimidating. Their conclusion is that Christmas is humbug.

Santa thinks humbug is just a funny word, but he won't critique his critics. He knows that believing in Santa Claus is as difficult as believing in yourself.

His reaction to centuries of cynicism has always been amusement—human beings are comical creatures. Santa knows that when he surprises the cynics at home, they melt like icicles in the sun.

Some people will wink and whisper in your ear,
"Who are you, really?"

Tell them the truth.

You are really Santa Claus.

NICK KELSH is a renowned photographer whose work has been featured in numerous publications. He collaborated with author Anna Quindlen to create the best-selling books *Naked Babies* and *Siblings* (PenguinStudio), and is the author of STC's *How to Photograph Your Baby* and *How to Photograph Your Family*.

ACKNOWLEDGMENTS

Thanks to Bill Marr and Sarah Leen at Open Books, Kevin Monko, Michael Butler, Ken Fuson, Dave Blazek, Capa's Costumes, Sam Winward, Andy Parsons, Eric Kelsh, Chaz Kelsh, George and Linda Morgan, James Marr, Morris Finkle, Henry and Katharine Medina, Dan, Lois, and Emily Cook, the Conants, the Egnaczyks, the Marrleen New Year's Eve party guests, Marisa Bulzone and Kim Tyner, the Fargo Theater, the Landis Valley Museum in Lancaster, PA, and all of the Santas in Philadelphia.

But mostly to Anne, for loving me.

Photo of the author by Chaz Kelsh
Photo of the Fargo Theater by Dave Wallis

Copyright © 2001 by Nick Kelsh
All rights reserved. No portion of this book may be reproduced, stored in a retrieval system, or transmitted in any form or by any means, mechanical, electronic, photocopying, recording, or otherwise, without written permission from the publisher.

Published in 2001 by
Stewart, Tabori & Chang
A company of La Martinière Groupe
115 West 18th Street
New York, NY 10011

Library of Congress
Cataloging-in-Publication Data is available for this title.
ISBN 1-58479-089-X

Edited by Marisa Bulzone
Design by Bill Marr
Graphic production by Kim Tyner

Printed and bound in Hong Kong
by C&C Offset
10 9 8 7 6 5 4